A Series on Chinese Espionage

Vol I.

Operations and Tactics

NICHOLAS EFTIMIADES

VITRUVIAN PRESS

Portions of this text first appeared in the article. "On the Question of Chinese Espionage." The Brown Journal of World Affairs, Brown University, 20 Feb, 2020.

DEDICATION

To Richard W. Marsh, II. The most brilliant critical thinker, scholar, military historian, delivery man, and restaurant owner I ever knew.
R.I.P.

To the hard working men and women of the Federal Bureau of Investigation, Department of Homeland Security, and Defense Counterintelligence and Security Agency. Without fanfare they stand on the front lines of freedom against tyranny and oppression.

A Series on Chinese Espionage: Operations and Tactics

CONTENTS

PREFACE

This work reflects years of collecting, compiling, collating, and analyzing hundreds of China's foreign intelligence operations. Also included are documentary sources, media reports, and my experience from previous publications having done thousands of hours of research and interviews of Chinese intelligence officers, diplomats, defectors, and recruited assets.

What is not in this document is at least as important as what is. The focus of this work is on worldwide human intelligence (HUMINT) operations. It does not include China's intelligence analysis capabilities, technical collection, nor domestic operations against perceived internal threats. Also, cyber espionage is only addressed in select cases which were enabled by humans providing insider access.

It should also be obvious that this study reflects only known intelligence operations. Even with a review of hundreds of espionage cases there remain basic questions. For example, how many people are spying worldwide on behalf of the Chinese government? Do the hundreds of cases in this work represent 90 percent of the total or 10 percent? Every good counterintelligence officer would start out asking these questions. I do not know the answer and neither does anyone else. Intelligence services including those of the Chinese government do not know given China's decentralized 'whole of society' approach to intelligence collection. Yet the volume of cases and careful analysis of operational details allows us to draw certain conclusions about China's espionage operations and tactics.

Please note that on the last page of this monograph you will find a link and password to my video on An Analysis of China's Economic Espionage Operations and Tactics.

Key Findings

This report presents findings from analysis of 595 documented cases of China's worldwide intelligence collection efforts. Significant findings are as follows:

1. China has greatly expanded its espionage efforts over the last 20 years.
2. Chinese entities conducting espionage include government agencies, People's Liberation Army, State Owned Enterprises, private companies, individuals, and several universities.
3. Nearly half of China's worldwide collection efforts target military and space technologies.
4. More than 90 percent of these espionage activities are done by ethnic Chinese. Over 80 percent are done by males.
5. The Ministry of State Security (MSS) uses social media to target foreigners with access to sensitive information. The quality of recruitment attempts varies considerably.
6. The MSS uses China's visa and border control system to identify potential recruitments and manage clandestine assets.
7. MSS espionage tradecraft has improved over the last four years, at least partially in response to US counterintelligence efforts.
8. Almost half of China's traditional espionage efforts (political and military secrets) and covert action campaigns are targeted against Taiwan.
9. China's foreign science and technology collection efforts correlate closely to the priority technologies identified in government strategic planning documents, *Made in China 2025, Space Science and Technology in China*, and *A Road-map to 2050, the National Key Technologies R&D Program, and the 13th Five Year Plan.*
10. China's 'whole of society' approach to espionage negatively affects America's economy, diplomatic influence, and military capabilities. In addition, China's actions threaten European national and economic security through espionage and coercion against government entities and business decision making.

Introduction

Throughout recorded history, nations have employed the use of spies to support foreign policy goals and military operations. However, intelligence and related activities are normally relegated to the shadows and rarely subject to public review. While often employed to support foreign policy, such clandestine activities rarely become the subject of foreign policy. And yet, this is the case for the People's Republic of China with massive 'whole-of-society' approach to conducting espionage. This approach is creating a new paradigm on how intelligence activities are conducted, viewed, and addressed by nations. In fact, a key element in the US-China trade war and downward spiral in relations is Washington's demands that Beijing cease stealing American intellectual property and trade secrets. China denies the claim, but hundreds of recently prosecuted espionage cases prove otherwise. China's espionage activities are changing the global balance of power, impacting the US and foreign economies, and providing challenges to domestic, national security, and foreign policy formulation.

While the practice of espionage in China dates back to the Xia people (2070 BC - 1600 BC) the practice of state sponsored commercial espionage to collect Western technology was first recorded during the period of foreign dominance in the later part of the Qing Dynasty (1636-1912 AD). In his book *Records of Sea Power States,* scholar Wei Yuan sought ways for China to regain its wealth and power by collecting information on foreign powers and "learning from foreign technology and countering foreign countries with their technology."

China is not the only country[i] to historically engage in such practices. Russia, Iran and even some US allies engage in systematic, government-sponsored (trade secrets, intellectual property theft) and technology theft.[ii] Many governments, companies, and individual entrepreneurs violate US laws in the drive to possess or sell America's technology, government and corporate secrets. Violating a country's laws is common practice in the murky world of espionage. Almost every time an intelligence service conducts espionage in another country, it violates that country's laws, and that includes US intelligence operating overseas. The difference is that the US and many other nations conduct intelligence activities to determine and counter hostile or potentially hostile adversaries, not to develop their own industries or transfer foreign wealth. In contrast, much of the PRC's is focused on developing China's industries and transferring foreign wealth.

Analytical Methodology

One could analyze some small number of espionage cases and make general statements about the intelligence service, operational methodology, and collection objectives. In the case of China, one cannot simply look at a small number of espionage cases and hope to understand if, and how, the nation state is conducting espionage over a broad range of participating organizations throughout society. That type of understanding takes evidence based on detailed analysis of a sufficient body of data. Over the last ten years, I compiled and analyzed 595 cases of Chinese espionage that have occurred worldwide. More than 450 of those cases have occurred since the year 2000. Detailed analysis of these cases provides ample evidence that the PRC is conducting espionage as well as promoting and supporting espionage in its academic and private sectors. The analysis shows what organizations are responsible, their information objectives, gaps in their knowledge, and operational "tradecraft" techniques.

There is a wide variance in what the media, public, and US legal codes consider espionage. Five US statutes and administrative regulations encompass those definitions ((Espionage, (Export violations ITAR, EAR, IEEPA)), Covert Action, and Research violations)).[iii] For the purposes of this study, all the aforementioned legal definitions of criminal acts are categorized as 'espionage'. This definition of espionage considers media and common public usage, and similarities in the acts, i.e. conducting illegal acts in a clandestine manner at the direction of, or for the benefit of, a foreign government or entity. Chinese cyber espionage has generally not been included in this study. Select cases were included: 1. if they were done jointly with HUMINT operations, or 2. if the alleged perpetrator was identified by name in criminal complaints or indictments.

China's Legal Framework for Espionage

The CCP uses all elements of society to support its global espionage efforts. For example, all Chinese government departments are required to support Ministry of State Security (MSS) intelligence operations when asked.[iv] This simple policy provides China's intelligence apparatus the ability to leverage universities, think tanks, foreign affairs departments, government sponsored overseas educational programs, military liaison programs, friendship and student associations, etc. This policy provides access to many foreign government officials, scientists, academics, and students.

In addition to its use of government bodies, the CCP has molded China's legal system to ensure the intelligence apparatus can exploit private industry to gain access to foreign individuals, secrets, and technology. The CCP promulgated several laws in recent years that require companies and individuals to actively support China's intelligence activities. In 2014, 2015, and 2017, the National People's Congress and State Council made public the requirements that all Chinese citizens and companies (operating in China or Chinese companies abroad) must collaborate in gathering intelligence.

Article 22 of the 2014 Counter-Espionage Law (反间谍法) states that during a counter-espionage investigation, 'relevant organizations and individuals' must 'truthfully provide' information and 'must not refuse'[v].

Article 7 of China's National Intelligence Law (国家情报法) of 2017 (Passed by the National People's Congress) states that "Any organization or citizen shall support, assist and cooperate with the state intelligence work in accordance with the law, and keep the secrets of the national intelligence work known to the public.[vi] The state protects individuals and organizations that support, assist and cooperate with national intelligence work." In addition, Article 14 provides intelligence agencies authority to compel any entity to provide this support: "The state intelligence work organization shall carry out intelligence work according to law, and may require relevant organs, organizations and citizens to provide necessary support, assistance and cooperation."[vii]

In November 2017, Beijing published the National Intelligence Law Implementing Regulations explaining that "When state security organs carry out the tasks of counter-espionage work in accordance with the law, and citizens and organizations that are obliged to provide facilities or other assistance according to the law refuse to do so, this constitutes an intention to obstruct the state security organs from carrying out the tasks of counter-espionage work according to law".[viii]

Within Chinese society, companies and citizens are required to provide the government with intelligence -- if requested -- with severe punishments for noncompliance. The state also assures that it "shall protect individuals and organizations that support, cooperate with, and collaborate in national intelligence work."

In essence, Beijing's creativity and ability combine all the elements of 'societal power,' including espionage, information control, industrial policy, political and economic coercion, foreign policy, threat of military force, and technological strength to create the world's first 'digital authoritarian state.'

PRC Organizations Conducting Espionage

Espionage activities correlated to their sponsoring organization (the "customer" receiving the information or technology) showed five distinct clusters of organizations engaging in espionage. The governing CCP uses government, quasi-government, academic, and commercial entities as mechanisms to conduct all forms espionage abroad. Most interesting of these are China's 'non-traditional collectors' which include State Owned Enterprises, universities, and private companies. The employment of such a broad set of entities for intelligence collection indicates China's 'whole of society' approach to espionage.

1. China's Ministry of State Security -China's preeminent civilian intelligence agency is the *Guojia Anquan Bu*, or Ministry of State Security (MSS). The MSS was formed in June 1983 by combining the espionage, counterintelligence, and security

functions of the Ministry of Public Security and the Investigations Department of the Chinese Communist Party Central Committee.[ix]

2. Central Military Commission (CMC) Joint Staff Department, Intelligence Bureau (formerly 2 PLA). -Responsible for collecting and analyzing foreign military intelligence including technology. People's Liberation Army (PLA) collection capabilities include military attaches conducting overt and clandestine collection, students, and other collectors under government and commercial covers.[x] [xi]

3. State Owned Enterprises (SOE) -There are 150,000 SOEs in China; 50,000 of which are owned by the central government and include aerospace and defense companies, subordinate research institutes, and technology transfer organizations. The State Council's State Assets Supervision and Administration Commission directly manages 102 of these firms considered critical to national and economic security. The CCP's Organization Department makes all senior personnel appointments within these business organizations.[xii] CCP embedded committees manage all actions within directly managed SOEs. In 2018, Xi Jinping directed all SOEs to amend their bylaws to ensure the concepts of service to the CCP -- national and economic security -- are placed above profit.[xiii]

4. Private companies and individuals. In approximately 22 percent of cases, PRC companies or individuals were acting unilaterally for commercial benefit only. In some of those cases (perhaps 30 percent), there was a clearly identifiable PRC government, SOE, or university as the ultimate customer for illegal exports or trade secrets. SOE involvement was most often apparent in illegal export of military technology, source code, large-scale agricultural and industrial production, and manufacturing techniques.[xiv] University involvement is often in establishing shadow labs to copy foreign research and commercial production facilities to replicate foreign material and technology.

5. Other PRC government elements that collect intelligence (information) and technology include the PLA Political

Department Liaison Office (targeted against Taiwan), United Front Work Department (UFWD) and many universities under the State Administration for Science, Technology, and Industry for National Defense (SASTIND).[xv]

Housed under the China's State Council, SASTIND assigns research projects to ministries with military production responsibilities. It manages military acquisition requirements for the Central Military Commission's Equipment Department. Ministries pass the work to the research institutes under their auspices, and the associated research institutes send their information and technology gaps back to SASTIND.

Within SASTIND there are two departments responsible for developing and tasking technology related intelligence requirements, and for collecting intelligence against those requirements. Those departments are the Comprehensive Planning Department and the International Cooperation Department. The Comprehensive Planning Department tasks collection to the MSS and most likely, the PLA, Joint Intelligence Bureau. The International Cooperation Department has its own independent collection capability. Members of this department travel with PRC scientists to collect information against specific requirements.[xvi]

SASTIND also has direct supervision over seven universities as well as contracts for defense research with 55 additional universities. The seven universities are called the Seven Sons of National Defense. Several of them have been identified in US court documents as actively conducting espionage, working with the MSS to conduct espionage, or receiving stolen foreign research and technology. Several of these universities have high security research facilities to support classified technology development for the PLA. The Beijing University of Aeronautics and Astronautics is also on the US Department of Commerce Entities List for their research in support of Chinese defense entities involved in the theft of technologies.

- Beijing Institute of Technology
- Beijing University of Aeronautics and Astronautics*
- Harbin Engineering University *
- Harbin Institute of Technology*

- Northwestern Polytechnical University *

- Nanjing Aeronautics and Astronautics University *

- Nanjing University of Science and Technology[xvii]

In total, over 35 Chinese universities (or professors from these universities) are identified in US court documents as having some role in China's overseas espionage cases.[xviii]

PRC Organizations Conducting Espionage

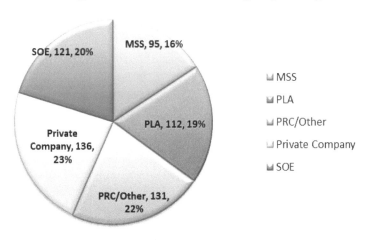

Figure 1. Chinese Organizational Clusters Committing Espionage

The distribution of Chinese espionage cases worldwide illustrates the magnitude of CCP controlled businesses, research entities, and government organizations involved in espionage activities (*See figure 1.*). There is a near equal distribution of espionage activities between the four major organizational clusters (MSS, SOE, PLA, Private Companies). This distribution indicates a concerted effort to use all mechanisms of government and the economy to collect foreign information and technology. Thus far, neither the CCP nor the Chinese government has taken any measures to impede illegal activities (according to the foreign countries' laws) of their state corporations, private businesses, universities, and citizens. Yet Beijing, as a 'digital authoritarian state' is clearly capable of doing so. Instead, the CCP views the appropriation of foreign innovations and technology as part of a policy aimed at developing domestic technology and increasing production.

The statistical breakdown of cases shows Chinese private companies have an aggressive posture in conducting espionage resulting in 136 cases or approximately 23 percent of all activity worldwide. Similarly, State Owned Enterprises are quite active in conducting or collecting information or technology in 121 cases or 20 percent of total. The SOEs are stealing primarily advanced military technology and associated research. Private companies and individuals target primarily commercial technologies, intellectual property, and military technologies. Espionage activities conducted by the People's Liberation Army, Joint Intelligence Bureau target primarily defense information, armaments, and military (or dual use) technology. [xix] The PLA was involved in 122 instances of espionage or 19 percent of all cases. The MSS was involved in 95 instances of espionage or 16 percent of all cases. MSS targets include political and defense information, foreign policy, overseas dissidents, military capabilities, and foreign intelligence services. The last categories of entities conducting espionage on behalf of the PRC are several Chinese Universities and the United Front Work Department. The universities target foreign technology to support advanced military weapons systems development and commercial endeavors.[xx]

Intelligence Collection Objectives

Intelligence terminology, Collection Objectives, also called Information Objectives or Requirements, identify the specific information (or technology) that is tasked for collection. These can number in the tens-of-thousands and reflect the nation's knowledge and technology gaps. For example, if a country is continually trying to collect information on specific components of turbine engines, it is because it lacks the required information or technology for its planned purposes.

The PRC identifies its strategic collection objectives in several national level planning documents. These documents do not openly task intelligence agencies or State Owned Enterprises.[xxi] They are, however, used as basis for China's collection – legal and otherwise – of foreign technology.

The national level strategic planning documents are further subdivided into specific technology development programs.

- National Basic Research Program (973 Program)
- National High-Tech Research and Development Program (863 Program)
- National Key Technologies R&D Program
- National S&T Major Projects
  - Advanced Digital Control Machines and Fundamental Manufacturing Equipment
  - Breeding of New Variety for Transgenic Biology
  - Core Electronic Devices, High-end General Chips and Fundamental Software
  - Key New Drug Innovation
  - Large-scale Development of Oil & Gas Fields and Coal-bed Gas
  - Mega-scale Integrated Circuit Manufacturing Technologies
  - Next Generation of Broadband Wireless Mobile Networks
  - Wastewater Control and Treatment
  - Agriculture S&T Achievement Industrialization
  - National New Products Program
  - National Soft Science Research Program

As one further breaks down the strategic technology objectives a strong correlation to China's espionage activities emerges. The Director of National Intelligence report, *Foreign Economic Espionage in Cyberspace* (2018) identified key industries and priority technologies that are frequent targets of foreign espionage. A subset of these data is shown in Figure 4. The top row identifies priority technology requirements in China's State Council 2015 strategic plan *Made in China 2025.* [xxii] The subsequent rows show specific technologies identified in espionage cases. These priority technologies are the targets of more than half of China's global economic espionage efforts. *(See Figure 2.)*

Collection Objectives and Espionage Cases

Clean Energy	Biotechnology	Aerospace & Ocean Engineering	Information Technology	Manufacturing
Clean Coal Technology	Agriculture Technology	Deep Sea Exploration	Artificial Intelligence	Robotics
Low Carbon Tech Production	Brain Science	Space Navigation Technology	Cloud Technology	Additive Manufacturing
Energy Storage Systems	Genomics	Next Generation Aviation Equipment	Information Security	Advanced (nano) Manufacturing
Hydro Turbine Tech	Precision Medicine	Satellite Technology	IoT Infrastructure	New Materials
New Energy Vehicle	Genetically Modified Seeds	Proximity Ops Technology	Semiconductor Technology	Smart (AI) Manufacturing
Nuclear Technology	Regenerative Medicine	Arctic Technology	Quantum Computing	Green Manufacturing
Smart Grid Tech	Synthetic Biology	Precision Optics	Telecoms	
Power Technology	Pharmaceutical Technology	Heavy Launch Vehicle Technology	5G Technology	

Figure 2. Adapted from the Office of the Director of National Intelligence

An even closer correlation between China's espionage efforts and national requirements can be made when comparing the 595 cases with the 10 key technologies identified in the CCP's strategic industrial planning document *Made in China 2025*. These technology requirements were the primary collection objectives in 435 cases. The fact that such a high proportion of espionage activities are correlated to the *Made in China 2025* key technology list indicates CCP guidance of the global espionage effort. *(See Figure 3.)*

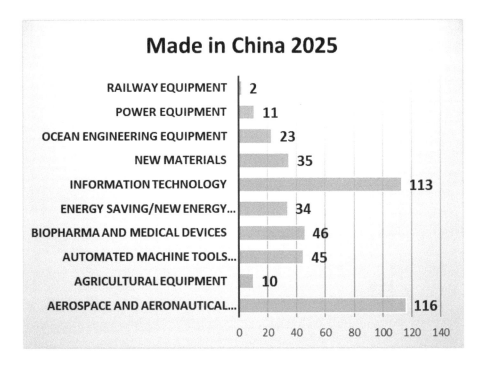

Figure 3. Made in China 2025

The data in Figure 3. clearly show that China puts a strong collection emphasis on foreign aerospace and aeronautical equipment (116 cases). Approximately half of those collection activities are targeted against military aerospace technologies. State Owned Enterprises and the PLA are the primary customers for foreign aerospace technologies, related trade secrets, and intellectual property. The primary collectors are the PLA Joint Intelligence Bureau and private companies conducting export violations, and individuals (Insider Threats) working in foreign aerospace companies.

The Ministry of State Security is also actively engaged in stealing foreign aerospace technology. Several cases illustrate the MSS involvement in HUMINT[xxiii] espionage as well as using contract cyber hackers to steal foreign aerospace technology.[xxiv] In at least two cases these were joint operations leveraging individuals inside an aerospace company to target it for cyber-attacks. These collection efforts support PLA military aerospace programs and China's commercial aviation sector.

A review of the 116 espionage cases targeted at aerospace companies identified over 200 specific military and civilian technologies and trade secrets (stolen or attempted stolen). Key technologies included: Cryogenic pumps for space vehicles, valves, transfer lines, refrigeration equipment, space qualified radiation hardened circuits, components for the storage and use of liquid hydrogen, cryogenic coolers, Ka-band space communications, satellite/missile insulation blankets - germanium coated polyimide film, and multi octave travelling wave tubes used as amplifiers in satellite transponders. Major systems include the Space Shuttle, Delta IV Rocket, F-15 Fighter, C-17 transport, F-22 Fighter, F-35 Fighter, B-1 Bomber, Ch 46/47 Chinook, C-130 training equipment and much more.

Another high priority PRC collection target is information technology. China's collection of information technology (113 cases) is second in numbers only to aerospace technology. China has placed strong emphasis on stealing information technology to include advanced semiconductors and manufacturing technology. In 2015 Beijing started allocating $50 billion dollars for the domestic development of advanced integrated chips. This action is intended to ensure self-reliance after the US began restricting semiconductor sales to the Chinese company ZTE. The US sanctioned ZTE for evading sanctions on Iran and North Korea and repeatedly lying to Department of Commerce officials. The US subsequently lifted the order three months later when the company paid a $1 billion fine and agreed to reprimand its Board and cut their bonuses (which it never did). The Chinese company Huawei is under similar export restrictions for evading sanctions on Iran and its theft of US technology. Huawei personnel face charges of economic espionage or espionage in the United States, Germany, and Poland.

China does not yet have the manufacturing technology to produce certain categories of advanced semiconductors to include radiation hardened chips. This manufacturing technology has as its core element, several methods of etching laser lithography chips at a nano scale. In a 2019 case, the FBI arrested Hu Anming, an associate professor at the University of Tennessee, Knoxville for wire fraud and lying on federal documents while working on a NASA contract. Hu allegedly established and managed a 'shadow laboratory' at Beijing University of Technology Institute of Laser Engineering developing the exact same technology.[xxv]

Key information technology related collection objectives include microelectronics, microwave integrated circuits, microprocessors, circuit boards, crypto key devices, data and voice transmission systems, semiconductors, and trade secrets such as laser manufacturing techniques. Semiconductor manufacturing is critical for China as the US and several other nations still maintain quite a lead over China in production capabilities. As a result, it is a primary collection objective for the PRC.

Other priority targets for collection include biopharma and medical devices, automated machine tools and robotics, energy saving/new energy vehicles, and new materials development. There are often distinct patterns of intelligence activity that correspond to each category of technology. For example, excluding PRC cyber espionage campaigns, collection on biopharma and medical devices is limited to exploiting research programs (e.g. Thousand Talents Program) or economic espionage using company insiders. The three targets for this category are universities, research institutes, and pharmaceutical companies.

In the category of energy saving/new energy vehicles most of the collection activity has been economic espionage employing insiders. The two targets for this collection effort have been companies and research laboratories. Most thefts of this technology have occurred through insider threats with cyber espionage as a secondary method.

Analysis of Espionage Cases

The dominant activities for China's overseas espionage are economic espionage, espionage, and export administration regulation (dual use) violations; together comprising 60 percent of all activities. Taken as a whole, illegal exports (theft of dual use and military technology) make up approximately 47 percent of China's espionage activities abroad. When divided into the categories -- espionage, economic espionage, ITAR, EAR, IEEPA, covert action, research violations -- the 595 espionage cases show the percentages of operations as follows (*figure 4.*).

China's main espionage activities in the United States are the illegal export of military and dual use technology.[xxvi] These categories include (in the US) IEEPA, EAR, and ITAR violations and together these and other export related violations make up 43.7 percent (260) of all cases globally. Over 80 percent of those cases occurred in the US. *(figure 4.)*.

Economic espionage, which is mainly conducted by private companies or individuals, makes up 25.98 percent (119 total) of cases. The category of "traditional espionage" can be seen at 22 percent (108 total) of worldwide activities. However, the figure is 55 cases when Taiwan is removed as a PRC intelligence target. In terms of numbers of exposed cases, Taiwan is the single highest priority target for traditional espionage.[xxvii]

The distribution of espionage cases in the US shows the venue of the criminal act (i.e. where the crime occurred).[xxviii] (*See figure 5.*) The distribution pattern shows activity concentrations occurring in high tech sectors, manufacturing hubs, and business centers.[xxix] For example, northern California is home to 'Silicon Valley' and the number one spot in the US for China's illegal technology collection efforts. Over half of the 140 cases that occurred in California targeted technology firms in the northern part of the state. The other cases centered around San Diego and then Los Angeles.

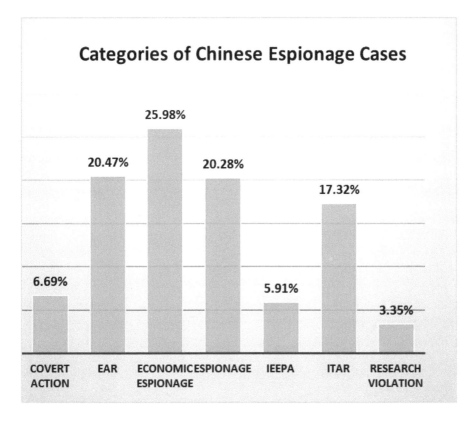

Figure 4. Categories of Chinese Espionage

Most of the collection activity in California was economic espionage (51 cases), EAR violations (30 cases), ITAR violations (25 cases), and IEEPA violations (13 cases).[xxx] In the economic espionage cases, the predominant form of tradecraft was using insiders (employees) to access restricted technology and trade secrets. The priority collection objectives in California were information technology (46 cases), aerospace and aeronautical equipment (27 cases), and automated machine tools and robotics (20 cases).

China's collection activities cluster around the major educational, research, and manufacturing centers in several states to include Massachusetts, Michigan, New York, Pennsylvania, Florida, New Jersey, and Texas. Victims of China's espionage efforts in the US include major defense and aerospace companies, pharmaceutical firms, technology research companies, and manufacturers.

In cases in Virginia and Florida, PRC diplomats and citizens also trespassed on military facilities to conduct ground photo reconnaissance. The facilities were associated with US naval forces and special operations capabilities.

Research universities are also primary targets for collection efforts most often accomplished through talent programs (i.e. Thousand Talents Program, Hundred Talents Program, etc.). Most estimates suggest there are at least 200 Chinese talent programs designed to employ academic and professional expertise from the West into serving China's national development. This expertise ranges from scientific and engineering fields to business, finance, and social sciences. These programs are serviced by 600 overseas stations that gather information on foreign scientists and then attempts to recruit them.[xxxi] In numerous cases, professors, graduate students, and PLA researchers have also been arrested stealing research from overseas universities for use in China.

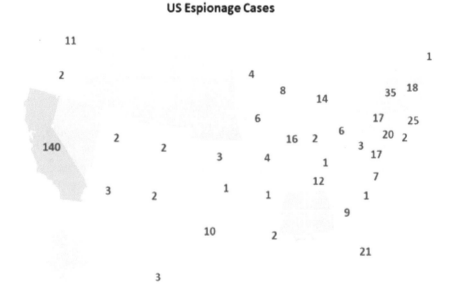

Figure 5. Distribution of Chinese Espionage Cases in the United States

Analysis of Espionage Tradecraft

Interesting aspects of the PRC's overseas espionage activities include their use of specific clandestine collection techniques commonly known as tradecraft. Chinese government agencies, State Owned Enterprises, companies, and individuals employ varying levels of sophistication of espionage tradecraft. An analysis of operational details reveals six specific patterns in tradecraft practices:

- Cyber espionage[xxxii]
- HUMINT enabled cyber espionage
- No tradecraft using open communications and true names.
- Use of false names and/or third parties to transmit information and ship materials.
- Public and commercial encryption, hosting meetings in China to avoid detection.
- Tailor made devices or techniques (i.e. dead drops, covert communications),[xxxiii] use of third countries for meetings, use of in-country cutouts to transmit information. *(See figure 6. Tradecraft Overview.)*

As illustrated, the most frequently employed elements of tradecraft include using false names or documents to illegally collect and ship information or technology. These techniques were used more than one third of the time (198 cases) and most often employed in EAR, ITAR and other violations. The false names and documents include use of front companies, email and bank accounts, end user certificates, identity documents, certifications, and falsified shipping documents. It should be noted that the use of false PRC government documents, ease of moving items through customs, and the involvement of universities and use of government facilities indicates some level of official support from the PRC.

In approximately 15 percent (88) of cases, individuals employed some form of commercial encryption for communications and/or hosted meetings in China to avoid detection by law enforcement or counterintelligence agencies. In these cases, the use of encryption was limited to commercial software applications and does not include bespoke sophisticated applications designed to mask the use of encryption software. Such covert communications (COVCOM) applications are often employed by intelligence services when necessary.[xxxiv] The negative aspects of using this form of communication is that a recruited asset or the communications channel could be compromised by a foreign counterintelligence service. If so, the foreign counterintelligence service could spend years monitoring the relationship or even feeding Beijing false information.

China's intelligence services prefer meetings in the PRC (and occasionally third countries) to avoid detection and compromise by law enforcement or counterintelligence services. Commercial encryption programs, meetings in China, and electronic communications were most often used to conduct Economic Espionage (18 USC 1831) and national security related espionage (18USC 790 series).

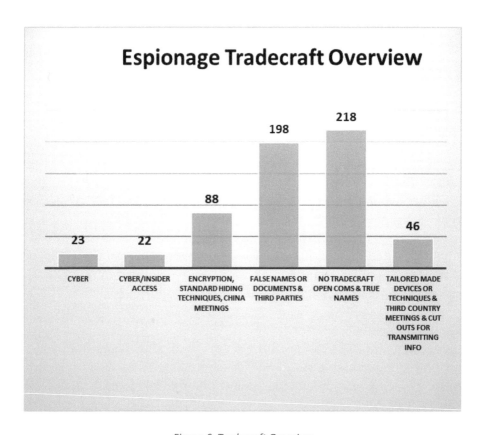

Figure 6. Tradecraft Overview

In 218 cases, the organizations and individuals involved used little or no tradecraft or did not make any significant attempts to hide the espionage activity. In these cases, individuals used true names and open communications including emails, text messages, and phone calls. These techniques were most often seen in insider threat scenarios, Thousand Talents Program research violations, and export violations. Lastly, in 46 cases, roughly eight percent of the total, PRC intelligence officers and/or recruited agents displayed a more sophisticated level of tradecraft. This tradecraft was almost exclusively used in conducting national security related espionage. These elements of tradecraft included specially designed smartphone software for secure covert communications,[xxxv] third country meetings, or use of third parties (cutouts) in the US for communicating information between the in-country 'handler" and recruited asset, or the in-country handler and PRC intelligence services.

Recent Espionage Cases

The wide variance in sophistication of espionage tradecraft implies the idea of "Islands of Excellence". This concept means the Chinese government and private entities employ espionage tradecraft with varying degrees of sophistication and effectiveness. One expects poor tradecraft from non-professional intelligence entities such as individuals, companies, and State Owned Enterprises. However, cases attributed to the Ministry of State Security show an astounding 24 cases where case officers and recruited agents demonstrated no discernible tradecraft. *(See figure 7.)* In these cases, persons conducted agent recruitment, tasking, communications, and data transfer openly, with no significant attempt to hide the activity. In another 13 cases, MSS operatives employed only simplistic or limited operational tradecraft. In only 14 cases was there a sophisticated higher level of tradecraft employed in operations. *(See figure 7.)*[xxxvi]

Figure 7. illustrates the variance of tradecraft used in Chin's espionage operations. One conclusion than can be drawn from these data is that the wide variance in professional tradecraft techniques likely indicates MSS suffers from lack of standardized training, operational security awareness, oversight, and case management. In addition, the same erratic performance by recruited agents illustrates non-standardized or limited agent training, protocols, and practices.[xxxvii]

The recent case of Xuehu 'Edward' Peng in 2019 provides insight into MSS operational tradecraft.[xxxviii] Specifically, the Peng case along with several others illustrates an evolution of tradecraft to higher levels of proficiency in certain areas. Peng was convicted in the United States for acting as a covert agent of the MSS. He was a support asset servicing dead drops between a recruited agent and MSS operations officers. The purported recruited agent was in fact in the service of the FBI, and therefore a 'double agent'. Several of these operational practices are consistent with other recent espionage cases.

1. This case represents the first time (publicly) the MSS used dead drops in the US.
2. The MSS identifies individuals in the US (travelling to the PRC) for potential recruitment as espionage assets. Peng and the FBI source were approached for recruitment while visiting China. The MSS was aware that the source had access to classified information, making him/her a recruitment target. These (successful) efforts identifying potential assets (for recruitment) indicate an extensive targeting effort integrated with the Chinese government's visa issuance and customs program.
3. MSS tradecraft is not effective in asset validation. Although the operation ran for two years the MSS was unable to detect the source was an FBI-controlled asset.
4. China uses official cover and non-official (government) for its intelligence officers (*note – they also make extensive use of non-government commercial cover).
5. China provides a minimal level of training in clandestine espionage tradecraft to its intelligence assets. Both Peng and the Source received some level of instruction (or at least direction) from MSS officers.
6. MSS officers in Beijing used ethno-nationalism as the motivation for Peng's recruitment.
7. Beijing based MSS officers handled the FBI source and Peng. Peng made numerous trips to the PRC carrying SD cards with classified information. Hand carrying information (often encrypted) to Beijing is common practice among intelligence assets.
8. MSS tradecraft employs intercontinental email and phone calls to communicate with assets using simple codes. The MSS may

have switched to encryption software with Peng as this was discussed, and the FBI noted a drop in phone communications shortly thereafter. Simple codes and open communications are common practices. Some recent cases have employed the use of encryption.[xxxix]

9. MSS tradecraft includes travelling to third countries to control assets working elsewhere. The FBI Source met with two MSS officers in Europe to reduce suspicion and increase operational security of the asset. This is a technique often used by MSS.

10. There is no indication that MSS practices include having controlled assets sign receipts. (* note – this makes their intelligence system ripe for corruption by allowing operations officers to skim payments).

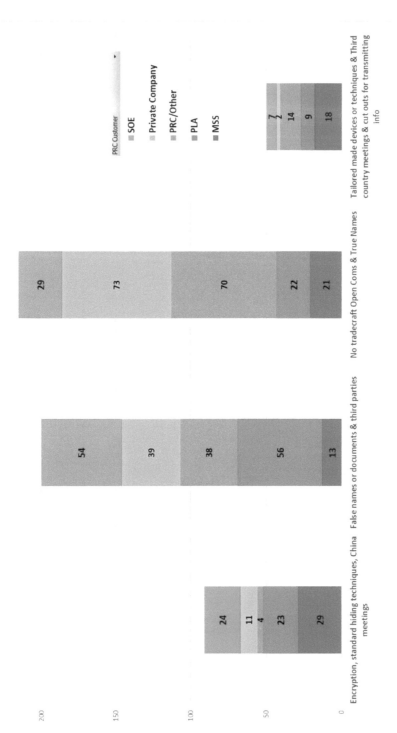

Figure 7. Espionage Tradecraft Techniques by Specific PRC Entities

11. Over the course of two years Peng did not detect FBI surveillance indicating no surveillance detection training or operational preparations.[xl]

Another recent case that provided insights into MSS operations is Jun Wei Yeo, also known as Dickson Yeo. Yeo was convicted by the United States in 2020 for covertly acting as an asset for the MSS. He was a Singaporean national and PhD student at the National University of Singapore. Yeo was a self-proclaimed Sinologist (China expert). He most likely came to the attention of the MSS due to his prolific online presence and pro-China views. He frequently made pro-China comments on online news sites such as The Diplomat and China-centric news blog "Shanghaiist" from as far back as 2010. Yeo also wrote more than 200 posts on the question and-answer site Quora (between 2014 and 2019). [xli]

Like Peng, Yeo was recruited during a trip to China, in Yeo's case to attend a conference. He was recruited by individuals claiming to work for a Shanghai based think tank.[xlii] Yeo established a fake consulting firm on the social media platform LinkedIn with the intent of identifying and recruiting Americans with Top Secret security clearances. Before being discovered and arrested, his efforts resulted in 400 resumes passed to Beijing with several targets in developmental stages of recruitment. Yeo's experiences show some parallels with the Edward Peng case:

1. The MSS used the PRC's visa system to identify Yeo as a recruitment target. After recruitment, MSS officers routinely escorted Yeo past customs lines to hide his travel to PRC. These actions illustrate a cooperative relationship between the MSS and visa/border control agencies.
2. PRC based MSS officers handled Yeo as a source. While he was recruited by the Shanghai State Security Department, he appears to have had multiple handlers from different provinces.
3. Yeo made numerous trips to China to provide information and to coordinate with Intelligence Officers.
4. The MSS provided Yeo with a minimal level of training in spotting and assessing individuals of interest (i.e. those who

were dissatisfied with work, having financial troubles, had child support issues, and developed good rapport with Yeo).

5. Yeo received the exact same tasking from all his PRC intelligence service contacts. If true, the conclusion is that one central authority in Beijing disseminated intelligence requirements to provincial level components.

6. The MSS instructed Yeo not to travel to the US with his phone or notebooks.

7. Yeo used the encrypted Chinese messaging application, WeChat. The MSS officers directed him to create a new WeChat account every time he connected with his Chinese intelligence handler and to use multiple phones. - The MSS instruction regarding WeChat is particularly noteworthy as China has recently publicly complained of US border agents searching the phones of select Chinese nationals.[xliii] The PRC embassy in Washington D.C. posted a website warning to Chinese citizens that their electronic devices are subject to being searched at US borders.[xliv] The PLA also appears to be taking that warning seriously as was evident in operational security measures in the case of Xin Wang. Wang is alleged to have lied on his visa application and is actually a PLA officer undercover in the US. Wang was arrested at Los Angeles International Airport for visa fraud. He had deleted the content of his WeChat service before arriving at the airport to return to China.

8. The MSS instructed Yeo that he should not send any email unless he was connected to the internet at a coffee shop. (*note – this instruction is designed to use a random IP address.)

One of the interesting aspects of the Dickson Yeo case was his use of Internet to target and then attempt to recruit individuals to conduct espionage. The US, Britain, Germany, and France have reported China targeting their nationals through LinkedIn. Recruitment approaches through LinkedIn appear to be MSS standard operational practice.

In 2018, the newspaper Le Figaro referenced a French intelligence report stating that the MSS had approached 4,000 individuals on LinkedIn..[xlv] Of that number, 1,700 are employed or integrally involved with French national institutions. Like the Yeo case, approaches are often subtle offering paid consultantships, free business trips to China, and other monetary incentives. In 2017, the German Federal Office for the Protection of the Constitution (BfV) reported the number of citizens identified by the MSS to be 10,000.[xlvi] According to the BfV report, the MSS was interested in 5 percent of those individuals. In the US, two former intelligence officers were recruited by the MSS through LinkedIn and at least 400 more identified as being of interest.

The use of LinkedIn and other social media platforms as recruitment aids is not unique to the MSS. It can be assumed many intelligence agencies follow this practice. What appears to be unique to the MSS is the volume of targeting and approaches. Through using social media in its operational tradecraft, the MSS can achieve the following:

1. Identify people with active security clearances, financial situation, personal likes, political views, their affiliations, contact data, and professional contacts within commercial, defense, scientific, and intelligence sectors.
2. Organizational structure, offices, roles, and responsibilities.
3. Use of social media platforms by intelligence services offers opportunities to send viruses through documents such as application forms, employment contracts, etc.

Another case that reveals MSS tradecraft is that of Yanjun Xu. In 2018, the FBI used a double agent to lure an MSS officer Yanjun Xu, (aka Qu Hui, aka Zhang Hui) to Belgium where he was arrested and extradited to the US for economic espionage . Xu was allegedly stealing aerospace technology. He was a Deputy Division Director with the MSS's Jiangsu State Security Department, Sixth Bureau. According to the FBI criminal complaint, Xu was using the Jiangsu Science & Technology Promotion Association as cover employment and working closely with the Nanjing University of Aeronautics and Astronautics. Xu also had contract cyber hackers working under his direction. Like Xu, these hackers were collecting foreign technology. The Xu case reveals yet more about MSS tradecraft:[xlvii]

- MSS Sixth Bureau officers are working at State Security Department (provincial level).

- Combines Cyber-HUMINT collection efforts indicating a very innovative and adaptive approach to tradecraft. In contrast, most other nations have separate agencies conducting HUMINT and cyber collection.
- Xu's HUMINT and cyber collections operations were targeting foreign technology indicating that the MSS Sixth Bureau is likely responsible for multi-discipline intelligence collection of foreign technology. There is conflicting data on this point that identifies the MSS 13th Bureau as being responsible for S&T collection.[xlviii]
- MSS provincially based State Security Departments target foreign technology and individuals and conduct HUMINT operations domestically and abroad. Yet, several MSS State Security Departments have been identified conducting cyber collection operations as well. The implications of these facts are as follows:
  a. MSS integrates cyber and HUMINT collection activities at provincial levels.
  b. The MSS has decentralized cyber collection through several provincial level SSDs. [xlix]
  c. Presumably, there is some level of centralized coordination through the MSS at the headquarters level. However, given the tremendous redundancy in operational targets, a central coordination of cyber collection appears weak at best. It is possible that provincial level SSDs are more in competition with each other to fulfill national level intelligence requirements.

Despite all the changes in tradecraft, on several occasions the FBI successfully dismantled operations and has even run double agents against the MSS. The success of the bureau's efforts in countering China's intelligence operations is clear evidence of MSS lack of operational security and weak practices in asset validation.[l] The US law enforcement response has resulted in providing strong evidence of Beijing's activities to include video tapes, recorded conversations, and a significant number of arrests and convictions.

It is not only the FBI who has been thwarting China's intelligence activities. Over the last five years counterintelligence and law enforcement services from the United Kingdom, France, Germany, Belgium, Poland, Australia, and Canada have thwarted espionage plots. In the US, the Department of Homeland Security (DHS) can also claim credit for disrupting many of China's numerous attempts to illegally export US military and dual use technology. The tradecraft in the Yeo and Peng cases along with PRC public warnings about US border security practices show attempts to lessen the vulnerabilities of intelligence operatives when passing through international border controls. Even Consul General Cai Wei of the (former) Houston Consulate was caught by DHS at George Bush International Airport along with two other Chinese diplomats using falsified birth certificates to escort Chinese students to the tarmac to board a chartered Air China flight.[li] Why the senior Chinese diplomats felt compelled to falsify information on their identity documents is unknown.

The MSS's overall mediocre performance in oversight and case management is possibly due to deficiencies in internal training, organization, and procedures. There appears to be little central authority or direction in managing provincial level offices. This lack of central management is illustrated by the fact that MSS operations worldwide show dramatic variances in clandestine tradecraft. In addition, several contractor cyber hacking groups working for MSS provincial level (state security bureaus) offices operate relatively independently with little or no apparent coordination. These offices have focused responsibilities for collection on specific geographical regions of the world. This division of responsibilities provides a greater weight of evidence to the assertion that there is lack of coordination and consistency in applied tradecraft.

The highly politicized nature of CCP management of the intelligence services also plays a role in the code of behavior and quality of intelligence. China's intelligence services have an exceptionally long history of suffering political purges at the hands of the CCP. The requirement to adhere to the CCP's preconceptions of the West is a limiting factor for China's intelligence collectors and analysts. There is, therefore, little incentive for analysts to present intelligence not consistent with the established status quo.

As a result of these limitations, MSS performance is not likely to significantly improve anytime soon. Indeed, a look at MSS tradecraft over the last 20 years shows recent improvements in targeting, recruitment, and operational agility (i.e. use of Internet, joint cyber and HUMINT). There has been some limited improvement in operational security. However, the overall service still suffers from the same long term systemic problems of politicization, lack of standardization, poor OPSEC, oversight, and mission overlap at provincial levels.

Analysis reveals several other interesting data points on the application of tradecraft. Private companies are the most likely to employ no or minimal tradecraft. In these collection activities, no tradecraft (41 cases) or minimal tradecraft (32 cases) was used in the conduct of operations. (See Figure 6.) The minimal use of tradecraft is expected, as these cases typically do not involve professional intelligence operatives (either operations officers or recruited agents). These cases usually fall into one of two categories:

1. Export violations conducted by PRC business or individuals using front companies in the United States or third countries (i.e. United Kingdom, Singapore, Hong Kong, Germany). The process involves lying to the manufacturer or seller about end use of products, not filing or filing false shipping papers, and mislabeling items (i.e. part numbers) to deceive Customs personnel.
2. Individuals acting as insider threats to US companies, academic or research institutions by stealing research, Intellectual Property, and Trade Secrets. In cases employing company insiders there is a vast variance in applied tradecraft. Most of the cases using no or minimum tradecraft occur just months before the insider announces plans to permanently return to China.[lii]

State Owned Enterprises' espionage activities show a wide variance in tradecraft as well. The operational details revealed in individual cases implies that this phenomenon is due to the following factors:

1. Significant differences in the technical knowledge of the individuals selected to collect foreign technology.
2. No standardized (or more likely any) training program for handlers or recruited assets.
3. Differences among the various SOEs.

4. Variables of espionage targets to include military, space, dual use, energy, biomedical, and manufacturing industries.

What is consistent about the espionage methods used by SOEs is that they show greater appreciation for the need to maintain operational security and higher level of tradecraft. This may be because the large defense-related SOEs engaged in this effort are more closely controlled by the CCP.[liii] Such close control includes personnel management through the CCP Organization Department and an internal CCP committee to oversee company operations. In contrast to private companies, SOEs more often employed false names, false documents, and third parties to obfuscate illegal activities (54 cases). (See Figure 6.) They also employed commercial encryption and hosted meetings in China (24 cases) to avoid detection.

SOE cases show different levels of engagement in executing collection operations. For example, in the cases of Su Bin[liv] (convicted) and more recently Xiaoqing Zheng[lv] (pending) the defendants were literally shopping their stolen technology and trade secrets to SOEs at central and provincial levels.

Su Bin (Aka Stephen Su) was the owner and manager of Lode-Tech, a PRC based aviation technology company with an office in Canada where Su had established permanent residency. In this HUMINT enabled cyber operation Su worked with a three person team of PRC based cyber hackers to infiltrate and extract data from US and European aerospace companies. From 2009 – 2013, Su leveraged his company's extensive network of business contacts to target individuals with access to military aviation technologies providing emails, contact data, etc. to his cyber hacking team. When the team was successful at penetrating a company's computer network Su translated documents and guided the team on which technical data to steal.[lvi]

In a February 2012 report to PRC officials, members of the Su Bin team claimed to PRC officials success in penetrating Tibetan organizations, Taiwan's military, and in collecting US military and civilian aviation technologies. The US technologies included 32 military projects, hundreds of thousands of files, and more than one hundred gigabytes of data.[lvii] [lviii] In Su Bin's report he claimed that the information would "allow us to rapidly catch up with U.S. levels," and that the information was protected by U.S. export restrictions, and that it would allow them to stand easily on the giant's shoulders." [lix]

Su would also seek to sell stolen data obtained by his co-conspirators to entities in the PRC, including to state owned aircraft companies, for their personal profit. In fact, in several of the emails Su Bin exchanged with his conspirators, they justified the importance of their collection with Chinese aviation experts and complained that the state owned aircraft companies were "cheap" in paying for the information. [lx]

In 2019, the FBI charged Xiaoqing Zheng in New York, and Zhaoxi Zhang (Liaoning Province, China), with economic espionage and conspiring to steal General Electric's trade secrets on turbine technologies. [lxi] The Xiaoqing Zheng case shows similarities to that of Su Bin. The FBI's indictment alleges Zheng used a commercial software called AxCrypt to encrypt GE's technical files and integrate them digitally into a photograph with a process called steganography. The technical files included proprietary data involving design models, engineering drawings, configuration files, and material specifications associated with GE gas and steam turbines. Zheng then emailed an innocuous photo of a sunset with the data inside it. [lxii]

The FBI alleges that Zheng emailed many of the stolen GE files to his business partner and relative in China, Zhaoxi Zhang. The two used the stolen GE trade secrets to advance their own financial interests in two Chinese companies they had established - Liaoning Tianyi Aviation Technology Co., Ltd. and Nanjing Tianyi Avi Tech Co. Ltd.

Like Su Bin, Zheng traveled to China to advance his operational activity. Unlike Su, Zheng used operational security measures including steganography, encrypted text messages, and voice messages.

Zheng travelled to China to allegedly establish business partnerships based on his stolen technology. He met extensively with provincial level CCP officials and with several Party, government, and business leaders including the Presidents of the Aero Engine Corporation of China and the Aero Engine Academy of China. He also met with officials at Northwestern Polytechnical University, [lxiii] and the Shenyang Aeroengine Research Institute (i.e. the 606 Institute).

The two aforementioned cases illustrate China's whole of society approach to espionage. It is an entrepreneurial approach to conducting economic espionage which uses financial awards as incentive along with contributing to China's national development. The CCP and China's government develops, encourages, and supports these efforts.

In other cases, SOEs were more directly involved in the tasking and clandestine collection process.[lxiv] The varying levels of SOE involvement and the exploitation of individual 'entrepreneurs' to collect technology is evidence of China's whole of society approach to conducting espionage. The PRC's intelligence collection apparatus and capabilities range from government agencies, organizations, and commercial entities to individuals entrepreneurs, Chinese expats, and foreign researchers.

It should be noted that most of the people cooperating with the Chinese government to conduct espionage are not professional intelligence officers. What then causes these persons to risk violating the law and risking prison sentences? The primary motivations for individuals (entrepreneurs, Chinese expats, and foreign researchers) become apparent in reviewing the 595 cases:

1. Establishing a business. Much of the theft of technology and trade secrets is done to establish personal businesses.[lxv]
2. Money. Some individuals have received cash for their services.
3. Ethnonationalism. There is a frequently expressed desire to "help the motherland".
4. Academic appointments. Several research thefts are done to receive academic appointments in Chinese universities.

Whilst the CCP may not be in direct control of all the clandestine collection, it clearly tasks hundreds of organizations and encourages thousands more to conduct espionage and support China's economic development and security needs.

The Thousand Grains of Sand Theory

In 1988 an FBI official spoke to the media describing China's approach to espionage as a "Thousand Grains of Sand".

"We have always compared them to grains of sand," one FBI official said. "If grains of sand were intelligence targets, the Soviets would surface a submarine in the dead of night and send a small party to the beach to bring back several pails of sand. The Chinese would send 1,000 bathers to the beach in broad daylight and have each bather bring back one grain of sand." lxvi

Over the last three decades a few academic researchers have challenged this characterization, citing as evidence MSS espionage cases that apply standard tradecraft similar to that used by Western intelligence services. These cases are cited as evidence that the "The Thousand Grains of Sand" theory is incorrect and that China's espionage activities are similar to those conducted by the West.

The FBI is correct, and they are wrong. Evidence beyond any reasonable doubt has emerged over the last three decades that shows the CCP employs all entities and mechanisms at its disposal to conduct espionage. The cases employing professional espionage tradecraft are quite few when compared to China's overall collection effort. China's 'whole of society' approach has the following general characteristics:

1. The CCP oversees MSS and PLA collection efforts.
2. MSS and PLA collection efforts share similarities with the West in espionage tradecraft. As tradecraft evolves, these similarities have increased in recent years.
3. The State Council provides technology production requirements to SOE's. There is nothing to indicate that either the Stace Council or CCP 'tasks' SOE's to steal foreign technology. However, given the presence of embedded CCP Committees in SOE's, it is likely there is awareness (if not actual approval) of these collection efforts.
4. Many of the cases involving SOE's, universities, and private companies involved using government services (i.e. research labs, shipping, customs, false documents, government facilities, Party approvals, etc.) showing the PRC's official support of these efforts.

5. The CCP's loose coordination of collection activities on a massive scale causes redundancy in target selection and acquisition.

It would appear the "Thousand Grains of Sand" Theory is safe for now.

Impact

The impact of China's global espionage activities varies by country according to domestic technology levels, commercial, and security interests. In the case of the United States, the impact manifests itself primarily in three ways:

1. The impact on the US economy, including loss of jobs, market share, losses from counterfeit and pirated tangible goods, and software piracy.
2. The impact on national security, specifically freedom of navigation in the South China Seas and China's advanced weapons to mitigate US force projection capabilities.
3. Countering US global diplomacy and influence

Economic Impact

Determining the total impact of China's espionage on the economy of any country is difficult if not impossible. One would have to know China's full range of successful espionage (We only know the cases that resulted in public exposure.) activities to be able to determine loss of global market share as a result. A near impossible task without access to more data. However, determining the impact of theft of intellectual property in part due to espionage is more easily estimated.

In 2016, the Organization for Economic Cooperation and Development and the European Union's Intellectual Property Office used worldwide seizure statistics from 2013 to calculate that 63 percent of the world's pirated goods come from China.[lxvii] The US Report of the Commission on the Theft of American Intellectual Property updated in February 2017[lxviii] assessed this figure at 70 percent. If including Hong Kong, the PRC accounts for 87 percent of all counterfeit goods seized. In 2019, the annual cost to the world economy from Intellectual Property (IP) theft alone is estimated over $600 billion.

Based on seizure statistics, 82 percent of the counterfeit goods seized in the European Union are believed to come from China. That figure is 80 percent in Canada and 76 percent (if Hong Kong is included, 87%) in the U.S. The annual losses to the US from China's IP theft are estimated at $360 billion.

The theft of intellectual property and the production of counterfeit goods results in unfair competition for American companies. China's theft of trade secrets and manufacturing processes required to produce industrial products has resulted in the degradation of US industries that produce solar panels, wind turbine control software, steel manufacturing, autonomous vehicles, and semiconductor chips. This degradation of industrial capability has resulted in the loss of at least two million American jobs. In addition, the quality of counterfeit auto, plane, and industrial parts from China is often substandard significantly increasing in risk to American consumers and industry.

The theft of the intellectual property from foreign companies and the production of counterfeit goods supports China's economic development strategy. A US Senate report estimated this practice as contributing eight percent to China's GDP so there is little incentive to stop. Foreign companies operating in China complain that Beijing views the appropriation of foreign innovations as part of a policy mix aimed at developing domestic technology and production.

National Security Impact

The most important implication for US national security planners is the loss of military technological advantage. China's advances in weapons systems — including autonomous robotics, avionics, hypersonics, and naval systems — are based in part on technology stolen from the United States and certain allies. This massive and sustained espionage campaign combined with two decades of increased defense spending provided China's PLA navy and air force with substantial power projection capabilities throughout Southeast Asia. The PLA Navy has achieved anti-access, area denial capabilities against its neighbors who also claim territories in the South and East China Seas.[lxix]

One of the most important targets for Chinese espionage is US space capabilities. Several illegal export cases show a focus and aggressive campaign to collect technologies on advanced space optics, sensors, cryogenic coolers, composites, engine design, fabrication techniques, software, etc. These collection requirements and dozens more are identified in government documents *Made in China 2025,* and *Space Science and Technology in China: A Road-map to 2050.* Chinese defense planners consider space control a critical part of degrading US force projection capabilities in the South China Sea. In addition, as China's PLA Navy evolves into open ocean capabilities it must have over the horizon communications and targeting which requires its own space capabilities.

To maximize its national security space capabilities, in 2015 the PLA created a Strategic Support Force as its cyber, space, and electronic warfare branch. China is quickly becoming more capable in space and counterspace operations, eroding the US advantage in this contested, congested, and competitive environment. The increase in PLA capabilities is significant because of the US dependency on space capabilities for communications, economic strength, critical infrastructure safety and resiliency, and to project military power globally.[lxx]

China's espionage activities that result in its increased power projection capabilities have geopolitical implications throughout Asia. As China's offensive military power grows, it advances an assertive and coercive foreign policy that is changing the balance of power in Asia. China is now able to (and does) coerce, threaten, or employ military force to enforce its territorial claims in East and Southeast Asia.

China's aggressive intelligence and counterintelligence has also reduced US and allied intelligence capabilities making CCP plans and intensions more difficult to understand. Media reports state the US spy network in China was devastated around 2012. There is some question of how (and if) this occurred. But Beijing openly celebrated the imprisonment and execution of Chinese citizens they said had been serving US intelligence. Whatever means China used to become aware of US assets in place, the loss of intelligence would have been devastating to the United States.

Perhaps more devastating than the US intelligence losses was the Chinese penetration of the French General Directorate for External Security (French: Directoire Générale de la Sécurité Extérieure, DGSE). The DGSE is France's external intelligence service. In 2020, two former DGSE officers (and the spouse of one) were convicted in Paris for providing intelligence to China over ten (+) years.[lxxi]

Recruited in Beijing these two individuals continued to provide China with intelligence while stationed at DGSE headquarters in Paris. Being able to secure intelligence from headquarters level in a major power such as France is a significant achievement for any opposing intelligence service. In this case, these recruited assets would have provided China access to some DGSE intelligence and most likely intelligence from partner countries.[lxxii]

The penetration of the French DGSE is not the only success China's MSS can claim against foreign intelligence services. From 2019-2020, the US convicted several former Case Officers on spying for Beijing:[lxxiii]

1. Kevin Mallory, former DIA and CIA Case Officer.[lxxiv]
2. Ron Rockwell Hansen, former DIA Case Officer.
3. Jerry Lee, former CIA Case Officer.
4. Alexander Yuk Ching Ma, former CIA Case Officer. The FBI arrested MA in August 2020. He is scheduled to go to trial. Ma allegedly worked with a relative (also in the CIA) which the US attorney elected not to prosecute due to advanced age and health.

Over the last three years, MSS agents identified include several persons in Taiwan's government, military, and political parties, a Russian professor and government advisor, a German diplomat, a Chinese professor in Brussels, and a Polish cyber intelligence officer. All combined, it is quite likely that China has clear insights into the intelligence and diplomatic activities and policy positions of several prominent countries in Europe. The same could be said for Taiwan. The director of the FBI has publicly stated that the Bureau opens a new counterintelligence case involving China every 10 hours.[lxxv]

Impact on Diplomacy and Policy Formulation

China's covert influence activities have received global attention in recent years. Covert influence campaigns in Taiwan, New Zealand, and Australia resulted in those governments conducting investigations and passing laws designed to prevent China's subversive actions.[lxxvi lxxvii] The United States has begun to investigate certain PRC institutions and individuals for compliance with the Foreign Agents Registration Act. The Trump Administration has also limited the expansion of

China's communications platforms in the US contending they are used to collect personal data. Even some American academic institutions in the US and Canada have rebuffed Beijing's covert and coercive attempts to stifle any negative discussions about China's actions or the CCP. Princeton, Harvard, and others have taken actions to stop Beijing from monitoring Chinese students in American classrooms. There are still policy issues as there has been resistance by US universities to disclose their financial entanglements with the Chinese government and companies. As of August 2020, the Administration has taken actions to stop PLA officers from studying in the US and several bills in Congress targeting PRC espionage and covert influence are being considered.

It is difficult to assess the effectiveness of China's covert global influence campaigns on US and foreign political processes. Efforts covertly funding political candidates, universities, business, and policy initiatives in other countries have likely been successful. However, media exposure of these actions frequently has severe consequences on interstate relations and public opinion. China's covert influence campaigns are less likely to be successful in the American political apparatus due to the strong competition which includes lobbyists, citizens organizations, NGOs, media exposure, and voter opinion.[lxxviii]

China's actions and statements concerning the COVID-19 virus did little to improve the global image of Beijing. Despite Beijing's worldwide propaganda efforts, Pew opinion polls in the United States show a decline in favorable opinions of China. The European Union's perception has also turned downward. In the United States, the percentage of people with favorable opinions of China dropped over the last decade from the 50's to 26 percent in 2020.[lxxix]

Summary

China's 'whole of society' approach to espionage negatively affects America's economy, diplomatic influence, and military capabilities. The same impact can be seen on many Western democracies. The sheer volume of these activities overwhelms Western law enforcement and counterintelligence capabilities. As mentioned in the preface of this text, there is no way of knowing how many of China's espionage efforts are ongoing at any given point in time. However, given the volume of activity one can safely assume it is in the thousands.

As illustrated throughout this text, the primary targets (assessed by numbers of cases) of China's foreign intelligence collection are Western (and Japanese) commercial and military technologies and trade secrets. This means the primary targets for China's espionage efforts are commercial businesses, research institutes, and universities. They are also the most vulnerable targets of China's relentless collection effort. These entities also include components of US critical infrastructure which are slowly making efforts at hardening and resilience.

The US security apparatus including the Intelligence Community is not organized to protect American industries' secrets. It is far better at protecting its own secrets. The same can be said for most other technologically advanced Western (and Japan) countries. The obvious problem in this situation is that commercial industry and scientific research programs are primary targets for Chinese intelligence collection, and the most vulnerable ones as well.

In the US, the DHS and FBI are leading the effort to combat China's massive intelligence collection campaign. Both organizations have done excellent work in reducing Beijing's relentless efforts but there is still much more to be done. The FBI has made advances since 2018 to assist US industry and academia. DHS is also working aggressively to curtail illegal exports of advanced technology and those who steal scientific research. Other government agencies as well as a bipartisan effort in Congress will also be necessary to ensure national and economic security

Success in thwarting China's aggressive collection efforts will ultimately rest upon three factors:

1. The ability of the US law enforcement and intelligence apparatus to shift organizational culture and support private industry and academia.
2. The US developing a strategic campaign integrating all the elements of government and its allies.
3. The Congress passing laws to raise the cost of economic espionage to the CCP, Chinese companies, and individuals (i.e. visa restrictions, sanctions, investment restrictions, etc.).

As illustrated throughout this work, China's 'whole of society' approach to espionage has been quite successful thus far in defeating government and private industry organizations.

European countries, India, and Japan's efforts to restrain China's intelligence activities have been comparatively less apparent in public sources. A limited number of espionage arrests in India, Germany, France, Belgium, and Poland indicate those countries are now moving to counter China's global collection efforts. In addition, the PRC's public image is suffering worldwide as the French and German governments have made statements on China's aggressive espionage on social media, human rights issues, Covid-19 response, and Beijing's threats over trade.

It will take a concerted effort by an alliance of nations to bring the CCP's behavior into compliance with global norms and thwart China's whole of society approach to espionage.

About the Author

Nicholas Eftimiades is a professor at Penn State University, Homeland Security Program. He is a member of the graduate faculty teaching homeland security, intelligence, and national security policy. Mr. Eftimiades retired from a 34 year government career including employment in the CIA, the US Department of State, and Defense Intelligence Agency. He held positions in analysis, human and technical collection, and leadership.

Mr. Eftimiades has a long history of success as an innovator in the U.S. Intelligence Community. He is widely regarded for his expertise on China and national security space issues. He has testified before congressional committees on several occasions. He has considerable experience in managing intelligence programs, strategic security issues in Asia, and national security space issues.

Mr. Eftimiades has an M.S. in Strategic Intelligence, National Defense Intelligence College, and a B.A. in East Asian Studies, George Washington University. He authored books, reports, and several articles on China's intelligence methodology, national security, technology, and space issues. His book "Chinese Intelligence Operations" is an examination of the structure, operations, and methodology of the intelligence services of the People's Republic of China. It is widely regarded as the pioneering work in the field.

Mr. Eftimiades currently holds an appointment as a National Intelligence Council, Intelligence Community Associate. He also serves on the DoD Defense Science Board and DHS Homeland Security Advisory Council, Subcommittee on Economic Security.

[i] (2019, January). SUMMARY OF MAJOR U.S. EXPORT ENFORCEMENT, ECONOMIC ESPIONAGE, AND SANCTIONS-RELATED CRIMINAL CASES (January 2016 to the present: updated January 2019). Retrieved from https://www.justice.gov/nsd/page/file/1044446/download

[ii] (2018, July Retrieved from https://www.odni.gov/index.php/ncsc-newsroom/item/1889-2018-foreign-economic-espionage-in-cyberspace26). NCSC Releases 2018 Foreign Economic Espionage in Cyberspace Report.

[iii] Note the following statutes are US laws. Because this database is global it requires normalizing data for all countries.

1. Traditional espionage (18 USC 792-799): The practice of spying or using spies to obtain information about the plans and activities of a foreign government.
2. Economic Espionage Act of 1996: The theft of trade secrets that includes the intent to benefit a foreign entity or at least know that the offense will have that result.
3. Illegal Exports: This body of law and regulations includes the Export Administrative Regulations (EAR), the International Traffic in Arms Regulations (ITAR) and the International Emergency Economic Powers Act (IEEPA). Each of these documents authorizes the president to regulate international commerce due to a threat.
4. Covert Action, or Foreign Agents Registration Act in the US (18 USC 951). FARA requires that agents representing the interests of foreign powers in a "political or quasi-political capacity" must disclose their relationship with the foreign government and information about their activities and finances. Covert Action is carrying out these activities without disclosure and is intended to create a political effect and conceal the identity of a sponsor or permit plausible denial. First published in Eftimiades, N. (2018, November 29). Uncovering Chinese Espionage in the US. Retrieved from https://thediplomat.com/2018/11/uncovering-chinese-espionage-in-the-us/

[iv] Bloomberg Quick Takes "What we Know About China's Spy Agency", Karen Leigh, Bloomberg Editor. Jan 19, 2019, 2:00 minutes. https://www.youtube.com/watch?v=-l6N1XdtUBM

[v] (2015, July 2). China Enacts New National Security Law. Retrieved from https://www.cov.com/~/media/files/corporate/publications/2015/06/china_passes_new_national_security_law.pdf

[vi] (2015, July 2). China Enacts New National Security Law. Retrieved from https://www.cov.com/~/media/files/corporate/publications/2015/06/china_passes_new_national_security_law.pdf

[vii] (2017, June 27). National Intelligence Law of the People's Republic of China (Adopted at the 28th meeting of the Standing Committee of the 12th National People's Congress on June 27, 2017). Retrieved from http://cs.brown.edu/courses/csci1800/sources/2017_PRC_NationalIntelligenceLaw.pdf

[viii] (2017, December 9). Detailed Regulations for the PRC Counterespionage Law

(Rush Translation). Retrieved from https://www.madeirasecurity.com/detailed-regulations-for-the-prc-counterespionage-law-rush-translation/

[ix] Chinese Intelligence Operations, Eftimiades, Nicholas New York, NY; Taylor & Francis, 2016. ©1994, p 17

[x] (n.d.). Ministry of National Defense, People's Republic of China. Retrieved from http://eng.mod.gov.cn/cmc/index.htm

[xi] Mattis, P. (2017, March 3). China Reorients Strategic Military Intelligence. Retrieved from https://www.janes.com/images/assets/484/68484/China_reorients_strategic_military_intelligence_edit.pdf

[xii] Brødsgaard, K. E. (2018, March 5). Can China Keep Controlling Its SOEs? Retrieved from https://thediplomat.com/2018/03/can-china-keep-controlling-its-soes/

[xiii] (2018, July 20). Communist Party the top boss of China's state firms, Xi Jinping asserts in rare meeting. Retrieved from https://www.scmp.com/news/china/economy/article/2027407/communist-party-top-boss-chinas-state-firms-xi-jinping-asserts

[xiv] Eftimiades, N. (2018, November 29). Uncovering Chinese Espionage in the US. Retrieved from https://thediplomat.com/2018/11/uncovering-chinese-espionage-in-the-us/

[xv] Eftimiades, N. (2018, November 29). Uncovering Chinese Espionage in the US. Retrieved from https://thediplomat.com/2018/11/uncovering-chinese-espionage-in-the-us/

[xvi] Phone interview, my book, and web page.

[xvii] * - Note: identifies China's Seven Sons of National Defense universities that were identified in US court documents in espionage or export violation cases.

[xviii] Chinese universities have been identified in US criminal complaints and indictments. There are varying levels of culpability ranging from active participation to only known association was professors working there.

[xix] Cases where the PLA was known, or believed to be the end user – e.g. The PLA was assumed the ultimate end user or 'customer' if a weapon's system (e.g. TOW anti-tank system tube-launched, optically tracked, wireless-guided weapon system) was being illegally shipped to the PRC

[xx] See for example, United States v. Donfang "Greg" Chung, Case 8:08-cr-00024-CJC, 07/12/2009, p 8.   https://fas.org/irp/ops/ci/chung071609.pdf; and United States v. Xu Yanjun, (Pending) Case: 1:18-cr-00043-TSB, 04/04/2018 https://www.justice.gov/opa/press-release/file/1099876/download

[xxi] There is an official mechanism for tasking technology related intelligence collection objectives to the MSS and PLA through the State Council Science and Technology National Defense, Secretaries office. The source providing   information on their functions is a former PRC Ministry of Foreign Affairs officer who has worked extensively with those offices.

[xxii] (2015, July 25). Made in China 2025. Retrieved from http://www.cittadellascienza.it/cina/wp-content/uploads/2017/02/IoT-ONE-Made-in-China-2025.pdf

[xxiii] Human Intelligence sources.

[xxiv] For example, United States v. Stephen Subin; and United States vs. Yanjun Xu.

[xxv] "Researcher at University Arrested for Wire Fraud and Making False Statements About Affiliation with a Chinese University." The United States Department of Justice, The United States Department of Justice, 27 Feb. 2020, www.justice.gov/opa/pr/researcher-university-arrested-wire-fraud-and-making-false-statements-about-affiliation. Also, see criminal complaint, https://www.documentcloud.org/documents/6789026-USA-v-Hu.html

[xxvi] EAR, ITAR, IEEPA

[xxvii] There could be several reasons for this statistic including Taiwan's aggressive approach to counterintelligence (exposing more cases), proximity to the mainland, ease of collection operations given language, close cultural and business relations.

[xxviii] In several cases, illegal acts occurred across the country or in other countries. In those cases, the map location is the one where either the target is located or in which the prosecution occurred.

[xxix] Several cases which emanated from the PRC are shown as Washington D.C because that is where the prosecution occurred.

[xxx] The International Emergency Economic Powers Act (**IEEPA**), is a US federal law authorizing the president to regulate international commerce after declaring a national emergency in response to any unusual and extraordinary threat to the United States.

[xxxi] Joske, Alex. "Hunting the Phoenix." ASPI, Australian Strategic Policy Institute, 20 Aug. 2020, www.aspi.org.au/report/hunting-phoenix.

[xxxii] Note – Cyber cases reflect only those where an individual was identified and prosecuted in the U.S.

[xxxiii] The first time China's use of dead drops was the Edward Peng case 2019.

[xxxiv] United States vs. Kevin Patrick Mallory, Defendant. Criminal No. 1:17-CR-154, United States District Court for the Eastern District of Virginia Alexandria Division, July 26, 2018. https://www.justice.gov/opa/press-release/file/975671/download

[xxxv] (2017, July 7). United States v. Mallory. Retrieved from https://casetext.com/case/united-states-v-mallory-31

[xxxvi] Note This monograph was being written as the Alexander Yuk Ching Ma case (Case 1:20-mj-01016-DKW-RT) became public. That case also employed relatively sophisticated tradecraft.

[xxxvii] In intelligence terminology, an "agent" is a recruited asset based in the target country or traveling to it.

[xxxviii] Cite U.S. vs. Edward Peng, 2019

[xxxix] Kevin Mallory, Zheng etc.

[xl] There are many other conclusions that can be drawn from analysis of this and other espionage cases. I have elected to leave them out so as not to educate the MSS.

[xli] Ng, Charmaine. "Dickson Yeo's Digital Footprint: Glimpse into Political Views, Childhood, Personal Convictions." The Straits Times, 11 Aug. 2020, www.straitstimes.com/singapore/dickson-yeos-digital-footprint.

xlii Note Think tanks are a common cover for MSS officers. Convicted spy and former Case Officer Kevin Mallory was also recruited by a Shanghai Based Think Tank.

xliii Power, John. "More Chinese Nationals Searched at US Customs: Official Data." South China Morning Post, 5 Aug. 2020, www.scmp.com/news/china/article/3096206/more-chinese-nationals-searched-us-customs-government-data-shows.

xliv "Chinese Embassy Issues Reminder to Citizens over U.S. Border Customs Checks." China News Service Website - Headlines, Stories, Photos and Videos, China News, 25 May 2020, www.ecns.cn/news/society/2020-05-25/detail-ifzwqsxz6423149.shtml.

xlv Le_Figaro, Christophe Cornevin, and Jean Chichizola. "Les Révélations Du Figaro Sur Le Programme D'espionnage Chinois Qui Vise La France." Le Figaro.fr, Le Figaro, 22 Oct. 2018, www.lefigaro.fr/actualite-france/2018/10/22/01016-20181022ARTFIG00246-les-revelations-du-figaro-sur-le-programme-d-espionnage-chinois-qui-vise-la-france.php.

xlvi "BfV-Newsletter Nr. 4/2017 - Thema 5." Bundesamt Für Verfassungsschutz, Bundesamt Für Verfassungsschutz, 28 Dec. 2017, www.verfassungsschutz.de/de/oeffentlichkeitsarbeit/newsletter/newsletter-archive/bfv-newsletter-archiv/bfv-newsletter-2017-04-archiv/bfv-newsletter-2017-04-thema-05.

xlvii United States vs. Yanjun Xu. U.S. Department of Justice, United States District Court, Southern District of Ohio, Case No. 1:18-cr-00043-TSB, Filed 04/04/2018 https://www.justice.gov/opa/press-release/file/1099881/download

xlviii Kozy, Adam. "Two Birds, One STONE PANDA." CrowdStrike, CrowdStrike, 29 Mar. 2019, www.crowdstrike.com/blog/two-birds-one-stone-panda/.

xlix Investigations into China's cyber collection activities indicate collection efforts from the following State Security Departments: KRYPTONITE PANDA/APT40 – Hainan, TURBINE PANDA/APT26 – Jiangsu, STONE PANDA/APT10 – Tianjin, GOTHIC PANDA/APT3 – Guangdong. They targeted the same categories of technologies in Europe and the U.S. Also, PLA and SOEs worked with contractor hackers operating through Hong Kong that attacked US aerospace companies (United States v. Stephen Subin).

l Asset validation is a continuous process to ensure the integrity of recruited agents (assets). It is done to ensure a foreign intelligence service does not manipulate or turn an asset against a foreign intelligence service.

li Churchill, Owen. "Chinese Military Uses Houston Consulate to Steal Research, US Diplomat Says." South China Morning Post, 23 July 2020,

lii There are many more details on the behavior of insiders conducting industrial espionage on behalf of China.

liii These include 112 State Owned Enterprises identified by the CCP.

liv "Chinese National Pleads Guilty to Conspiring to Hack into U.S. Defense

Contractors' Systems to Steal Sensitive Military Information." The United States Department of Justice, 11 Aug. 2016, www.justice.gov/opa/pr/chinese-national-pleads-guilty-conspiring-hack-us-defense-contractors-systems-steal-sensitive.

lv "Former GE Engineer and Chinese Businessman Charged with Economic Espionage and Theft of GE's Trade Secrets." The United States Department of Justice, 23 Apr. 2019, www.justice.gov/opa/pr/former-ge-engineer-and-chinese-businessman-charged-economic-espionage-and-theft-ge-s-trade.

lvi "Su Bin - U.S. District Court - Complaint June 27, 2014." United States of America v. Su Bin, Criminal Complaint, Case No. 14-1318M , US District Court, Central District of California, 27 June 2014, www.documentcloud.org/documents/1216505-su-bin-u-s-district-court-complaint-june-27-2014.html.

lvii Ibid. p. 17.

lviii Penetrations of US companies (primarily Boeing) provided technical data on the F-35, F-22 fighter, and C-17 cargo aircraft.

lix Ibid. p. 45

lx Ibid. p.36

lxi In an unrelated case in 2018 MSS officer Yu Yangun Xu was also indicted for attempting to steal General Electric's trade secrets on turbine technology.

lxii UNITED STATES vs. ZHENG Xiaoqing and ZHANG Zhaoxi Indictment, Case 1:19-cr-00156-MAD, Filed 04/18/19 https://www.justice.gov/opa/press-release/file/1156521/download pp. 7,8

lxiii One of the Seven Sons of National Defense.

lxiv See for example, Donfang "Greg" Chung, "Former Boeing Engineer Convicted of Economic Espionage in Theft of Space Shuttle Secrets for China." The United States Department of Justice, 16 Sept. 2014, www.justice.gov/opa/pr/former-boeing-engineer-convicted-economic-espionage-theft-space-shuttle-secrets-china.

lxv * Note – Motivations are often mixed, but establishing a business is by far the number one motivation for conducting espionage. Also, in a Confucian based society such as China, education is highly respected so academic appointments are sought after positions.

lxvi Overend, William. "China Seen Using Close U.S. Ties for Espionage: California Activity Includes Theft of Technology and Surpasses That of Soviets, Experts Believe." Los Angeles Times, Los Angeles Times, 20 Nov. 1988, www.latimes.com/archives/la-xpm-1988-11-20-mn-463-story.html.

lxvii OECD/EUIPO (2016), Trade in Counterfeit and Pirated Goods: Mapping the Economic Impact, Illicit Trade, OECD Publishing, Paris, https://doi.org/10.1787/9789264252653-en.

lxviii (2013, May). The Commission on the Theft of American Intellectual Property. Retrieved from http://www.ipcommission.org/report/ip_commission_report_052213.pdf

lxix Eftimiades, N. (2018, December 4). The Impact of Chinese Espionage on the United States. Retrieved from https://thediplomat.com/2018/12/the-impact-of-chinese-espionage-on-the-united-states/

[lxx] Eftimiades, N. (2018, December 4). The Impact of Chinese Espionage on the United States. Retrieved from https://thediplomat.com/2018/12/the-impact-of-chinese-espionage-on-the-united-states/

[lxxi] The spouse was convicted only of using the money knowing its origin.

[lxxii] Intelligence services are primary targets for other hostile (and friendly) intelligence services due to the wealth of information they possess. This includes intelligence from sources and from foreign governments (liaison).

[lxxiii] A Case Officer is one who identifies, assess, and recruits foreign nationals to spy on behalf of a country. In these cases, the Case Officers were themselves recruited by China's Ministry of State Security.

[lxxiv] Kevin Mallory was a Chinese linguist (like me). We trained together for five months in Diplomatic Security Service and briefly worked together later in our careers. He had worked as a case officer in CIA and DIA.

[lxxv] Haynes, Danielle. "FBI Director: U.S. Counterintelligence Opens a Case on China Every 10 Hours." UPI, UPI, 7 July 2020, www.upi.com/Top_News/US/2020/07/07/FBI-director-US-counterintelligence-opens-a-case-on-China-every-10-hours/7841594149629/.

[lxxvi] Brady, A. M. (2019, January 8). Magic Weapons: China's political influence activities under Xi Jinping. Retrieved from https://www.wilsoncenter.org/article/magic-weapons-chinas-political-influence-activities-under-xi-jinping, 23 August, 2020

[lxxvii] (2018, May). CHINA AND THE AGE OF STRATEGIC RIVALRY: Highlights from an Academic Outreach Workshop. Canadian Security and Intelligence Service, https://www.canada.ca/content/dam/csis-scrs/documents/publications/CSIS-Academic-Outreach-China-report-May-2018-en.pdf

[lxxviii] (2020, August 08). Eftimiades, N. (2018, December 4). The Impact of Chinese Espionage on the United States. Retrieved from https://thediplomat.com/2018/12/the-impact-of-chinese-espionage-on-the-united-states/

[lxxix] (2020, August 08). U.S. Views of China Increasingly Negative Amid Coronavirus Outbreak. Retrieved from https://www.pewresearch.org/global/2020/04/21/u-s-views-of-china-increasingly-negative-amid-coronavirus-outbreak/

Included with this monograph is a 50 (+) minute video on "A Comparative China's Economic Espionage Tactics". The video can be found here:

https://www.shinobienterprises.com/video

PASSWORD: Shinobi-1

Printed in the USA
CPSIA information can be obtained
at www.ICGtesting.com
LVHW062209040124
768234LV00005B/22